Henry

Purcell

Te Deum and Jubilate Deo in D

Edited by Robert King

vocal score

MUSIC DEPARTMENT

OXFORD
UNIVERSITY PRESS

UNIVERSITY PRESS

Great Clarendon Street, Oxford OX2 6DP,
United Kingdom

Oxford University Press is a department of the University of Oxford.
It furthers the University's objective of excellence in research, scholarship,
and education by publishing worldwide. Oxford is a registered trade mark of
Oxford University Press in the UK and in certain other countries

ISBN 978–0–19–338589–4

Music originated in Sibelius
Printed in Great Britain on acid-free paper by
Halstan & Co. Ltd, Amersham, Bucks.

The orchestral score and parts are available on hire/rental
from the publisher's hire library.

Scoring: soloists, SSATB chorus,
2 tpt, vln 1, vln 2, vla, vc, opt. cb, organ,
and optional theorbo

Duration: *c*.20 minutes

PREFACE

Henry Purcell's substantial body of sacred music includes sixty-five full and verse anthems, nearly half of which include instrumental accompaniment, thirty-five wonderfully varied Devotional Songs that range in scale from single voice to full choir, a setting of the morning and evening canticles in B flat, a further evening service in G minor, and the substantial Te Deum and Jubilate Deo. The majority of this music was composed during the reign of King Charles II, mostly for performance in the Chapel Royal (where from 1682 Purcell held the position of organist) and, to a lesser extent, for Westminster Abbey (where Purcell had been appointed organist in 1679). The Te Deum and Jubilate Deo, however, was written in 1694 for the annual St Cecilia's Day celebrations. This regularly included both a church service and a concert (usually held at Stationers' Hall in the City of London) at which a newly composed ode in praise of music was performed. For the first celebration in 1683, Purcell composed *Welcome to all the pleasures*, and by 1694 he had added another three Cecilian odes, the largest of which, *Hail, bright Cecilia*, was performed at the 1692 festival. For the 1694 celebrations he produced a substantial setting of the Te Deum and Jubilate Deo, which was performed at the service in St Bride's church, Fleet Street. Purcell had not only a choir and soloists at his disposal, but also a string orchestra, to which he added two trumpets, providing greater scope to echo the often celebratory texts. But alongside the spacious visions of heaven and its choirs of angels, the texts also allow for moments of intimacy, providing Purcell with the ideal vehicle to display his consummate word-painting skills. For, away from the grandeur of the sections for full choir and orchestra and Purcell's brilliant displays of contrapuntal technique, it is perhaps in the chamber movements that we find the greatest jewels.

As is to be expected from a work that was written for an important occasion that would have been attended by most of London's musical establishment, the grandest sections of the Te Deum are spacious and expansive. Pictorialization abounds: the trio melismatically depict the angels crying aloud; two sopranos represent Cherubin and Seraphin; and the full forces enter for three repetitions of 'Holy'. Heaven and earth are contrasted, with the solo alto and tenor covering celestial matters, leaving the lone bass to reflect a more earthly state. The Trinity is pictured in matched pairs of voices, linked by a pair of solo violins; vocal melismas represent the infinite majesty of the Father, a pair of sopranos represents the Son, and the two alto voices represent the Holy Ghost. 'Thou art the King of Glory' is set to an extraordinary piece of double counterpoint, where two themes—one strongly rising, the other more rhythmic and falling—combine effortlessly in five parts, the trumpets blazing above the whole ensemble. One of the most remarkable moments of the work is the supplicatory 'O Lord, save thy people', where Purcell employs ardent repetitions of the word 'save'. But the finest moment is kept back: the two octave rising phrase 'and lift them up for ever' starts in the bass, transfers to the tenor, and is finally taken up by the alto, rising to the top of their register, creating one of the most glorious vocal phrases in baroque music. The centrepiece of the work, which finds Purcell at his most personal, is 'Vouchsafe, O Lord', set for the composer's much-favoured alto (countertenor) voice. It is a genuine plea from the heart, made all the more poignant with the realization that exactly a year later Purcell himself would be dead. Here is the composer at his profound best, piling up sequences and dissonances and pleading for mercy in the most ravishing vocal and string writing. The serenity with which the movement ends, coupled with the strong affirmation of the final chorus, suggests that this is one prayer that may be answered.

While in his setting of the Te Deum Purcell mostly utilizes quite short sections (not least of all because he has a substantial amount of text to set), in the shorter Jubilate Deo he achieves longer musical spans. The opening is an extended duet between alto and solo trumpet, but, once again, it is in the more pastoral sections that Purcell shines—the duet between soprano and alto 'Be ye sure that the Lord he is God' is an especially touching one in its simplicity, and Purcell's use of sequence and gentle harmony creates a section that is full of pathos. The somewhat austere four-part canon 'O go your way into his gates' is followed by an extended duet for alto and bass, and, again, the plea for mercy draws Purcell into particularly effective writing. In the Gloria Purcell demonstrates his mastery of contrapuntal techniques: first the theme is treated to close imitation ('Glory be to the Father'), then it is inverted and imitated ('Glory be to the Son'), and finally, at 'world without end', a new theme is added, which is treated to the same techniques but also powerfully augmented in the bass. At the final Amen the strands come together and, with the trumpets soaring above the ensemble, a work of great technical and musical ingenuity ends in a blaze of sound.

ROBERT KING
Suffolk, 2012

Editorial practice

Purcell's own fair copy manuscripts are usually meticulously copied, containing very few errors, and even showing—quite unusually for the time—clear slurs to indicate precise placing of text syllables. It is therefore unfortunate that the original manuscript for a work of this importance is lost. Instead we turn to a printed copy published two years after Purcell's death by John Heptinstall for the composer's widow, Frances. Heptinstall's score is far from perfect, containing wrong notes, unclear underlay, and inconsistent textual slurs, as well as some uncertain musica ficta, all requiring editorial intervention. By all accounts, Mrs Purcell was short of money after her husband's premature death, so perhaps the edition was hurried out, or the copy supplied to the printer was not an original copy.

As with other editions in the *Classic Choral Works* series, the aim is first and foremost to serve the practical needs of non-specialist choirs, keeping the music pages as clean and uncluttered as possible, though not neglecting the needs of the scholar. Note values have been reduced to give a ♩ pulse; editorial barring has been shown in a modern, standard way; and key signatures have been modernized. Texts have been made consistent by reference to the 1662 Book of Common Prayer. Errors in the source that have been corrected are listed in this commentary. All material in square brackets or in small print is editorial. Full-size accidentals are those that appear in the source; they are silently omitted when made unnecessary by a modern key signature, and also omitted for immediate repetitions of the same note in the same bar. Small accidentals are editorial. Cautionary accidentals are shown full size in round brackets. Syllabic slurs in the voice parts are inconsistently indicated in the source. Those that are present have been retained, with judicious additions to create consistency; however, matching the source, longer melismas remain without slurs. Beaming and stemming of notes has been modernized. Editorial suggestions of tempo have been added to the keyboard reduction.

A keyboard part has been created in a playable form, without indicating every element of movement within individual polyphonic voices, especially where these cross. This sometimes results in apparent parallel fifths and octaves, but this is surely preferable to the frequent sight of upstems and downstems crossed. Where all the voices are impossible to play, the keyboard reduction has been discreetly simplified. In the continuo-only passages, an editorial continuo realization has been provided.

Instrumentation, pitch, and voice types

Purcell's orchestra at the Chapel Royal did not incorporate sixteen-foot instruments such as today's double bass. Instead, the bass line was played at eight-foot pitch by bass violins (larger versions of the cello, often tuned a tone lower to enable a low B♭). When performing this work, the number of first violins should be matched to the number of cellos (or bass violins, if available). There should be at least two cellos—one playing the solo sections, the other joining in the tuttis. The continuo section should certainly contain chamber organ and, ideally, at least one theorbo.

Performing pitch for most of the Chapel Royal repertoire was higher than that used today, probably around A = 466 Hz. The Te Deum and Jubilate Deo was written, however, for performance in St Bride's, Fleet Street, and evidence suggests that performing pitch there was probably a half-tone lower than today's pitch, at A = 415 Hz. In a performance using 'modern' instruments, modern concert pitch of A = 440 Hz will work satisfactorily; with period instruments, a pitch centred around A = 415 Hz will work best.

A frequent addition to Purcell's vocal ensemble was the 'high tenor' voice, which explains those Purcellian alto lines that sit uncomfortably low for falsettists. In the source, delineation between tenor and alto is clearly indicated by clefs (with C3 clef used for alto or high tenor, and C4 for tenor) and this edition follows that evidence. The choice of using alto or high tenor is editorial, based on the tessitura of the line. The ideal line-up for this work uses six soloists: two sopranos, alto, high tenor, tenor, and bass. Where a high tenor soloist is not available, this part should be sung by a second alto. A countertenor with a good lower register can usually take these lines, especially when the performance is at modern pitch.

Source and variants

Notes

1. Specific references to musical notes in the score are given thus: bar number (Arabic), stave number counting down from top stave in each system (Roman), symbol number in the bar (Arabic).

2. Pitch and rhythmic references are given in terms of the edition, not in terms of the original source. Where note values have been shortened, so have references to variants.

3. Corrections relevant only to instrumental lines are not listed in this vocal score, but are noted in the full score (available on hire/rental from the publisher).

Source: *Te Deum & Jubilate for Voices and Instruments, made for St Caecilia's Day, 1694 By the late Mr. Henry Purcell, London Printed by J. Heptinstall, for the Author's Widow . . . 1697* (British Library, IV 896 Hirsch)

Variants

Te Deum: 45 i 4: ♮ is editorial / 61 ii 3: source places syllable on previous note / 67 v 2: source shows 'Thy' / 103 i–iv 1: repeated 'all' is editorial / 107: original time signature $\frac{3}{2}$ / 124 i 3: source starts text slur one note too late / 140: original time signature ¢ / 152 iii 4: shown as f in source contrary to e in viola, here followed / 159: original time signature ¢ / 178 iii 8–9: notes reversed in source / 180: original time signature $\frac{3}{2}$ / 191: original time signature ¢ / 195 ii 3: source gives erroneous ♯ / 199: original time signature $\frac{3}{2}$ / 218 iii 1: source erroneously gives ♩ / 219 v 1: source gives ♩. / 231: original time signature ¢ / 254–7 iv: repeat of underlay is editorial / 261: original time signature ¢ / 279 ii 1–2: not tied in source / 289 iii 1: source erroneously prints d / 297 ii 4: upper voice last note shown as ♯ in source.

Jubilate Deo: 18 i 2: repeated 'all' is editorial / 33 v 3: ♯ is editorial / 34 ii & iii 3–4: rhythm dotted to match soprano and bass / 48 ii 3–4: rhythm dotted to match other vocal lines / 52 ii 3: source gives f, here altered to match trumpet line / 79 vi: source gives rhythm ♩ ♪♪ ♩ / 84 ii 1: source gives e / 85: original time signature ¢ / 102 ii 1–5: source underlay incongruously allocates four note melisma to 'the' / 140: original time signature ¢ / 141 ii 3: source missing tie / 145 ii 1: source indicates repeated 'gra-' (of 'gracious') at start of bar, contradicted in previous bar by a text hyphen / 170: original time signature ¢ / 186 i 2–3: source places text syllables one note further on / 196 iv 1: shown as ♩. in source / 201 iv 1: source gives b / 206 i: underlay position in source unclear / 213 ii 3–214 ii 1: source gives g / 218 i 1: source missing text syllable / 223–4 ii: text repetition editorial to match other voices.

Te Deum

Edited by
Robert King

HENRY PURCELL
(1659–95)

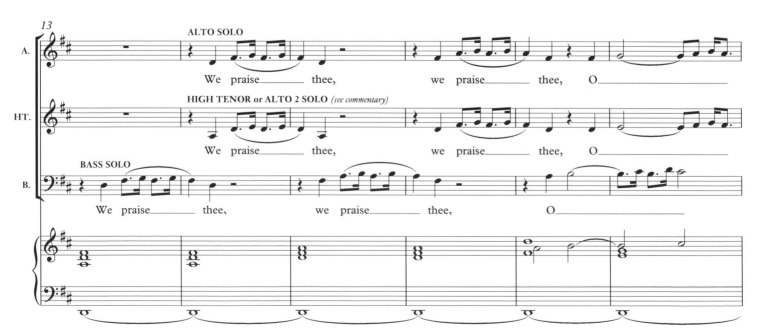

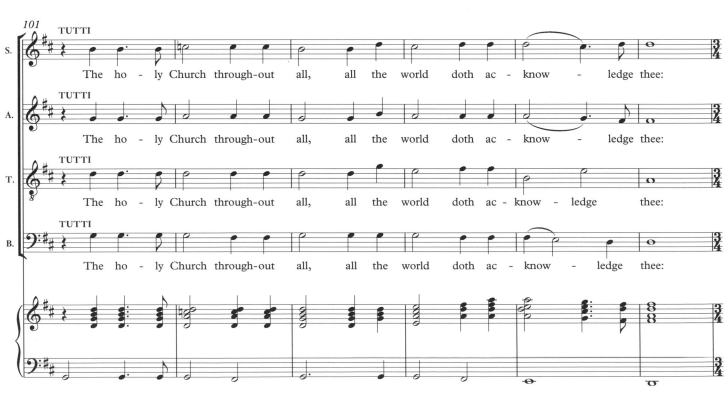

Jubilate Deo

Edited by
Robert King

HENRY PURCELL
(1659–95)

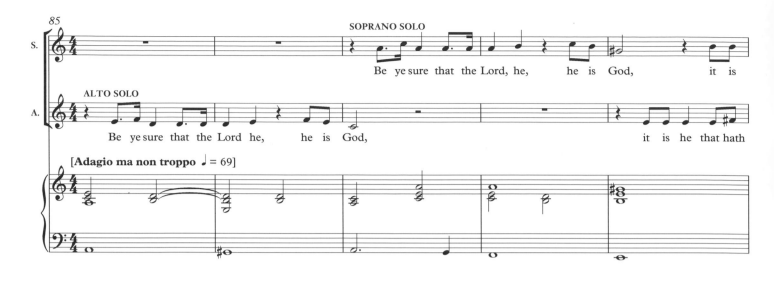